T0082955

HEALTHY AGING
FOR THE BRAIN

HEALTHY AGING FOR THE BRAIN

SHARMILLA KANAGASUNDRAM
AND MANVEEN KAUR

PARTRIDGE

Copyright © 2017 by Sharmilla Kanagasundram and Manveen Kaur.

ISBN: Softcover   978-1-5437-4418-7
                eBook   978-1-5437-4417-0

All rights reserved. No part of this book may be used or reproduced by any means, graphic, electronic, or mechanical, including photocopying, recording, taping or by any information storage retrieval system without the written permission of the author except in the case of brief quotations embodied in critical articles and reviews.

Because of the dynamic nature of the Internet, any web addresses or links contained in this book may have changed since publication and may no longer be valid. The views expressed in this work are solely those of the author and do not necessarily reflect the views of the publisher, and the publisher hereby disclaims any responsibility for them.

Print information available on the last page.

To order additional copies of this book, contact
Toll Free 800 101 2657 (Singapore)
Toll Free 1 800 81 7340 (Malaysia)
orders.singapore@partridgepublishing.com

www.partridgepublishing.com/singapore

CONTENTS

PROLOGUE

As medical science enjoys more and more successes, the number of people entering geriatric status will increase. Hence as psychiatrists we felt that attention needs to be directed toward healthy aging of the brain. Factors such as nutrition, comorbid medical illnesses as well as psychological stress need to be addressed as these, if modified can help retard aging changes taking place in the brain. Dementia is a condition that affects the brain in older individuals. Surprisingly the type of food we consume as well as how we manage stress can ascertain if this condition can be prevented.

In the day bygone, scant attention was paid to nutrition. Nutrition was viewed as being either from the group of carbohydrate, proteins or fats. In addition to its contribution by way of vitamins and minerals. Aging has always been seen as inevitable and a part of normal physiology. In fact we know that aging begins from the time we are born. As science becomes more molecular, and the knowledge and understanding of the underlying basis of aging deepens, we see that nutrition which was not seen previously as a therapeutic tool may actually be able to contribute to the prevention or retardation of human aging states. Retarding aging through food intake is a processes that may have been previously deemed not possible.

In this book we will elaborate on the beneficial effects that green tea has on the brain in terms of prevention of Alzheimer's disease as well as improving some aspects of cognition. We will also see how psychological stress promotes cognitive impairment through its action on the hippocampus.

INTRODUCTION

Aging is influenced mostly by genetic makeup, life style choices, and environmental factors. As we can see there are some modifiable factors. Non genetic factors contribute to 50-75% of the rate of physiological aging (Perls and Puca 2002). Many researchers have studied the influence of nutrition especially supplements on aging (William J, Miline JS 1978). Many studies have documented that supplements can help slow down the aging process. Such supplements that are useful to well- being of our brain are, fish oils and ginko biloba (Isah T et al 2015).

In this book we aim to identify the factors that contribute to aging and best methods to stop, delay or reverse the aging process with respect to the brain. We can broadly divide this into biological methods and psychological methods. Special emphasis was placed on nutrition, especially green tea and the Mediterranean and Okinawa diet as a means to delay brain aging.

Biological methods to improve brain health

1) Nutrition

- Green tea
- Mediterranean and Okinawa Diet
- Resveratrol
- Fish Oil (Omega 3)

2) Exercise
3) Avoidance of Environmental Toxins
4) Avoidance of Gerontogens
   Avoiding Gerontogens

Psychological Methods
- Stress management
- Good Sleep

Aging of the brain results in poor functioning namely poor memory and poor executive function among many other deficits. This translates to poor quality of life as well as loss of independence.

CHAPTER 1

COGNITION AS A FUNCTION
OF THE BRAIN

Cognition is the other word for thinking. Thinking is a complex process that involves multiple components.

Components of Cognition

1) Awareness (Alertness or vigilance).
2) Memory (working memory, short term memory and long term memory, visual and auditory).
3) Attention and concentration.
4) Executive capacity. (Planning, organizing, sequencing and abstraction)
5) Reasoning, problem solving and judgement.
6) Learning
7) Production of language.
8) Processing (Auditory and visual)

1) Awareness

Being aware is also known as being alert or vigilant. This function is brought about by the reticular activating system. Being aware of the surroundings is essential to thinking process.

2) Memory

Working Memory

Working memory consists of functions such as protection from external distraction also known as distractor resistance. Distractor resistance or intrusion resistance entails the prevention of exterraneous stimuli from intruding into working memory. In addition shifting attention within working memory and updating information are other components of working memory (Derek et al 2015).

Short term memory

Short-term memory short term memory is the temporary storage of information in the absence of more information and is essential in enabling higher-level cognition (Derek et al 2014).

Long term memory

Long-term memory is again divided into two types (Dudai 2002). Explicit (or declarative) memory and implicit (or procedural) memory Declarative memory/ explicit memory refers to those memories that are recalled at will (Dudai 2002). Declarative memory can be further sub-divided into episodic memory and semantic memory. (Dudai 2002). Procedural memory or implicit memory is associated with memory of skills of how to do things and it may be performed without being conscious of the action, such as tying a tie, playing a piano or dancing. These memories are typically enabled by repetition and much practice, and consists of automatic sensorimotor behaviors that are deeply embedded in our minds (Dudai 2002).

These "body/procedural memories" enable the carrying out of various ordinary motor actions more or less automatically Acquired skills like cycling are stored in the putamen, grooming behaviors are stored in the caudate nucleus while timing and coordination of body skills involve the cerebellum. Without the medial temporal lobe, one can still produce new procedural memories (such as playing the violin, for example), but will be unable to remember the other events during which it happened (Dudai 2002).

3) Attention and Concentration

Attention is the ability to maintain focus(Vyas and Shree Ram 2015). Within the reticular activating system, the thalamus plays an important role in the shifts in the focus of attention(Vyas and Shree Ram 2015). The thalami and cerebral cortex receive incoming sensory signals, evaluate the contents, and employ brain resources to accommodate the requests made. The thalami receives the information that comes through our senses, then relays it to the proper areas of the brain. Concentration is the ability to shift that focus from topic to topic (Vyas and Shree Ram 2015).

4) Executive Function

Executive function refers namely to planning, organizing sequencing of events and abstract thinking. This action takes part in the prefrontal cortex of the brain. This function appears to decline in dementia. (Vyas and Shree Ram 2015).

5) Judgement, Reasoning and Problem solving

Judgement is the product of the ability to reason.

6) Learning

Learning is the ability of humans to assimilate new information, or modify and enhance, existing knowledge, behaviors, skills. Learning encompasses skills such as integrating different pieces of knowledge.

The act of learning is a learning curve and does not happen at once, but builds on itself and collects on prior knowledge. Learning may occur as part of education, personal development, training and even through experience. Sometimes it is goal-oriented and is propelled by motivation. The study of learning behavior is known as educational psychology, Learning may occur as a result of habituation or classical conditioning. It can occur as a result of more complex activities such as play, and may occur consciously or without conscious awareness.

7) Production of language.

The various stages occurring in the creation of language encompass the following: The intended message, encoding the message into linguistic form, encode linguistic form into speech, then the sound goes from speaker's mouth to hearer's ear and the auditory system Speech is decoded into linguistic form and lastly the linguistic sound is decoded into meaning (Randi 2014).

8) Auditory and visual Processing

Auditory and visual processing disorders are neurological disorders that produce problems of perception in the face of normal and intact auditory and visual pathways. Individuals with auditory processing disorder cannot understand the information they hear in the same way as others do, which leads to difficulties in recognizing and understanding auditory stimuli, especially the sounds which are speech. Apparently these problems arise from dysfunction in the central nervous system.

Cognitive Areas of The Brain

a) Dorsolateral Prefrontal Cortex

The prefrontal cortex (pfc) is the most evolved part of the brain. It occupies the front third of the brain, underneath the forehead. It is often divided into three sections:

1) Dorsal lateral section (on the outside surface of the pfc),
2) Inferior orbital section (on the front undersurface of the brain).
3) Cingulate gyrus (which runs through the middle of the frontal lobes). Cingulate gyrus, is also considered as part of the limbic system. The dorsal lateral and inferior orbital gyrus are often termed the executive control center of the brain.

Functions of prefrontal cortex are summarized as below -attention span, concentration, perseverance, planning, organizing, judgment, impulse control self-monitoring and supervision, problem solving, critical thinking, forward thinking, learning from experience and mistakes, ability to feel and express emotions influences the limbic system, empathy, internal supervision.

b) Hippocampus

The hippocampus is a small area of the brain that is shaped like a sea horse and forms part of the limbic system. The limbic system is situated in the medial temporal lobe near the center of the brain. The other parts of the limbic system are the mamillary bodies and the amygdala. The hippocampus is associated with long memory especially declarative memory (Dudai2002) and spatial navigation. Declarative memory is that type of memory that is concerned with knowledge or facts. The hippocampus is not concerned with short tem memory. Short term memory is managed by the cerebellum as is procedural memory.

c) Basal Ganglia

A collection of nuclei known as the basal ganglia are found on both sides of the thalamus. Glutamate and GABA are the neurotransmitters here. The corpus striatum is made up of the caudate nucleus, the putamen, the globus pallidus, and the nucleus accumbens. The caudate begins just behind the frontal lobe and curves back towards the occipital lobe. It sends information to the frontal lobes. The putamen is situated under and behind the caudate nucleus. The putamen is involved in coordinating automatic behaviors such as bike riding and driving. The putamen and caudate play a part in procedural memory(Dudai et al 2002). The globus pallidus is located just inside the putamen, and has two parts, outer part and inner part. It receives inputs from the caudate and putamen and provides outputs to the substantia nigra (below). The nucleus accumbens is situated inferior to the globus pallidus. It receives signals from the prefrontal cortex through the ventral tegmental area and sends other signals back there through the globus pallidus. The substantia niagra is situated at the upper portion of the midbrain and below the thalamus, it is black due to deposition of the pigment neuromelanin. One part of the substantia niagra uses dopamine neurons to send signals up to the striatum. It is believed to be involved in the reward system.

d) Cerebellum

The cerebellum is located posteriorly. The cerebellum appears like an extra structure attached to the base of the brain. It fits neatly underneath the cerebral hemispheres. Its exterior is covered with finely spaced grooves different from the broad convolutions found in the cerebral cortex. The external surface of the cerebellum resembles an accordian.

It is involved in cognitive operations especially procedural memory as well as short term memory (Dudai et al 2002). In addition other operations like attention and language, and in regulating fear and pleasure responses are also cerebellar functions. However its motor functions are well established. While the cerebellum does not initiate movement, it helps in coordination, precision, and accurate timing. It receives information from sensory systems of the spinal cord and from various parts of the brain, and integrates these information to delicate motor functions. Damage to cerebellum produces disorders in fine movement, balance, posture, and motor learning.

e) Reticular activating system

The reticular activating system consists of loosely related neurons that are located at the brainstem that project in to the cortex through the thalamus. It functions to switch a person's conscious state from relaxed to highly attentive. It has ascending fibres known as ARAS or ascending reticular activating system. (Dudai et al 2002).

f) Thalamaus

The thalamus is a small structure that is located above the brainstem and below the cerebral cortex. The thalamus checks in-comming sensory information, and decides which is most important, and allows only the most important information access to higher brain levels (Dudai et al 2002)

CHAPTER 2

---- ☙ ----

ROLE OF NUTRITION IN PREVENTION OF AGING

GREEN TEA

Originating from East, tea is one of the most favored beverage over the last few centuries (Zhen 2002). Tea was first introduced to Japan in the 17 th century(Chako et al 2010). 2.5million tons are produced every year all over the world (Chako et al 2010). Tea is mainly enjoyed in Asia, United State and Europe (Chako et al 2010).

There are 3 basic tea, black tea, green tea and oolong tea. All the different types of tea come from the same plant Camelia Sinesis. Tea can be generally classified into 6 groups but the most studied are green, black and Ooolong tea(Tze Pin et al 2008). This classification stems from the extent of fermentation and oxidation of polyphenols in fresh leaves (Tze Pin et al 2008). Black tea is fully fermented, Oolong tea is partially fermented and green tea is unfermented.

Components of green tea are

Polyphenols
Amino acids
Methylxanthine

a) Polyphenols

Polyphenols make up 30% of the dry weight of tea leaves (Chako et al 2010). Polyphenols are subdivided into flavonols (catechins), flavandiols, flavonoids and phenolic acids(Chako 2010) and are the most abundant contents of green tea (Harbowy et al 1997) There are close to 30,000 polyphenolic compounds in green tea. Flavonoids attract the most attention as they have the most antioxidants effects (Harbowy et al 1997). The major flavanols (catechins) in tea are as mentioned below in the coloured box. (Dominc B et al 2015, Reygaert 2014):

FLAVANOLS

- catechin (C),
- epicatechin (EC),
- epicatechin gallate (ECG),
- gallocatechin (GC),
- epigallocatechin (EGC),
- epigallocatechin gallate (EGCG).

EGCG is the most active of these catechins and is often the subject of studies with respect to tea antioxidants. EGCG is found in abundance in the old leaves which contain more of the substance than green tea (young leaves) and oolong tea (Yung Sheng Lin et al 2003). Black tea contains less than green tea (young leaves) and oolong tea (Yung Shen Lin et al 2003).

Mechnism Of Action Of Polyphenols

1) Catechins, found in green tea are acknowledged to be potent antioxidants and hence provide beneficial health effects by protecting the body from the damaging effects of oxidative damage from free radicals (Susana et al 2006).

2) Catechins also help in the prevention of formation of abnormal alpha –beta proteins that are an important constituent of neuritc plaques of Alzheimer's Disease (AD). Epigallocatechin-3-galleate

(EGCG) is protective against beta amyloid induced neurotoxicity by inducing the formation of non amylodogenic soluble form of amyloid precursor protein. Thus amyloid plaques that are the cardinal feature of Alzheimers dementia are not formed (Kuriyama et al 2006).

FUNCTION OF POLYPHENOLS

1) ANTIOXIDANT ACTIVITY
2) PREVENTION OF AMYLOID PLAQUES

---

b) Amino Acids

The brothiness of tea is produced by the amino acids contained in the tea. Amino acids are more abundant in black rather than white tea. L-Theanine is the most abundant amino acid in green tea and constitutes, 50% of amino acid present in green tea (Ota et al 2014). L theanine constitutes 1-3% of dry weight and the median amount of L theanine per cup is 8-30 mg(de Mejia et al 2009). L-theanine has many chemical names, including gamma-glutamylethylamide and 5-N-ethyl-glutamine.

Mechanism Of Action Of L Theanine.

Up regulation of neurotransmitters

Theanine increases or up regulates serotonin, dopamine, GABA, and glycine levels in various areas of the brain (Nathan et al2006, Yamada et al 2007, Yokogoshi et al 1998, Wakabayashi et al 2012). They are neurotransmitters in the brain that are essential for the proper working of the brain.

Increases brain derived neurotrophic factor.

Theanine increases BDNF in certain areas of the brain (Lardner et al 2014). BDNF is a protein in the brain that promotes regeneration, differentiation and maintenance of neurons. BDNF is related to neurotrophin family of growth factors. It is synthesized by the dorsal horns and is up regulated in injury.

Promotes alpha activity

Theanine is known to promote alpha brain wave activity which promotes relaxation (Nobre et al 2008). In addition changes in alpha wave activity can bring about increase in selective attention during mental tasks.

NMDA dependent CA 1 – long term potentiation (LTP).

Improvements in learning and memory are brought about through an NMDA dependent CA 1 – long term potentiation (LTP).

Prepulse inhibition and sensorimotor gating.

The term sensory gating describes a neurological processes of removing unnecessary input to the brain. (Cromwell et al 2008). Prepulse inhibition (PPI) is a type of weak stimulus that takes place as a pre-attentive process and originates from the cortico -striato-thalamic-pontine-circuitary (Ota et al 2014). PPI has been proposed as a type of sensorimotor gating (Swerdlow et al 2009). PPI is deranged in schizophrenics (Swerdlow et al 2009). This impairment to filter out environmental stimuli contributes to both positive and negative symptoms of the schizophrenia. PPI is changeable following treatment with the N-methyl-Daspartat (NMDA) receptor antagonist.

FUNCTIONS OF AMINO ACIDS ARE

Up regulation of neurotransmitters
Increases brain derived neurotrophic factor.
Promotes alpha activity
NMDA dependent CA 1 – long term potentiation (LTP).
Prepulse Inhibition And Sensorimotor Gating.

c) Methylxanthine

Methyxanthine is the third most abundant compound in green tea. They include caffeine, theobromine and theoxanthine.

THREE IMPORTANT METHYLXANTHINES ARE
• **CAFFEINE** • **THEOPHYLLINE** • **THEOBROMINE**

Caffeine

The caffeine content in green tea is 15.3mg/100ml. Caffeine is a non selective A1 and A2a adenosine receptor antagonist that stimulates cholinergic neurons (Khokhar et al 2002). Caffeine content is more in black tea than oolong tea. It was also more in oolong tea than green tea. Processed green tea had more caffeine than a fresh tea leaf (Yung Sheng Lin et al 2003).

Theophylline

Theophylline, is also called 1, 3-dimethylxanthine (William M 1943), and it is a methylxanthine. This compound is used in therapy as a bronchodilator for chronic obstructive pulmonary disease (COPD) and asthma. It belongs to the xanthine family, and resembles structurally and pharmacologically theobromine and caffeine.

Theobromine

Theobromine tastes bitter and is an alkaloid from the cacao plant. It has the chemical formula $C_7H_8N_4O_2$ (William M 1943). Chocolate is rich in this compound. It is classified as a xanthine alkaloid. The degree of methylation makes one compound different from the other.

The central nervous stimulant qualities of xanthines are brought about their ability to enhance vigilance, attention, mood and arousal (Fisone et al 2004). It is an established fact that the effects exerted by methylxanthines depend on their capabilities to perform as antagonist at various adenosine receptors sites (Fredholm et al 1999). Adenosine is a ubiquitous neuromodulator acting at G-protein-coupled receptors namely A_1, A_{2A}, A_{2B} and A_3. The receptors most important in arousal performances are A_1 and A_{2A}.

d) Other constituents in green tea

- Carbohydrates- makes the tea sweet
- Minerals- arsenic, selenium, iodine, kalium, manganese, arsenic, nickel, fluorine, and aluminum.
- Pigments-chlorophylls and carotenoids
- Enzymes
- Volatiles

Antiaging effects of green tea on the brain can be measured by improvements in Mini Mental State Examination (MMSE).

The first MMSE was published in 1975 in a paper by Marshall F Folstein, his wife Susan Folstein and Paul Mc Hugh (Vyas and Shree Ram 2015). The Journal Psychiatric Research wrote about it as a series of questions marked on 30 points and was used frequently in research to measure if there was any defects in the cognition (Pangman et al 2000). It was initially utilized to differentiate organic (those illnesses due to a general medical condition) from functional (due to psychiatric causes) impairment (Folstein et al 1975, Tombaugh et al 1992). It is also being used a screening tool for dementia a degenerative disease of the brain (Vyas and Shree Ram 2015). The MMSE is used to assess how bad is the illness and progression over duration of time and can be used as a tool to show the effectiveness of treatment that is instituted.

Among the advantages of MMSE are that it requires no detailed training. It is both a valid and reliable scale. It takes only 10 minutes to do (Tuijl et al 2012). The MMSE can be used to differentiate between the different dementias. Those with Alzheimer's Disease score lower on orientation and recall compared to patients with Parkinson's, vascular or Lewy Body Dementia. Alzheimer's dementia is the most common dementia of all (Vyas and Shree Ram 2015).

Disadvantages of MMSE are that it is needs to be translated or interpreted into various languages, it is affected by chronological age and education standing. It also frequently fails to pick up minimal defects and cognitive deficiencies and it has only a few items that tests visuospatial ability (Tomburgh 1992).

A few mechanism may account for the beneficial effects brought about by green tea. Firstly studies show that tea can cause increased alertness, better accuracy in attentional switching and to a degree some unisensory and multisensory attentional improvements (Camfield et al 2014). Secondly tea has been known to increase fronto –parietal connectivity thus improving working memory. Possibly these are contributory features for the improvements noted by MMSE. Also these properties may retard the progression into dementia or MCI (Moeko 2014). Thirdly reduction in the production of beta amyloid induced toxicity also prevents amyloid plaques. Better MMSE results are obtained the more frequently green tea is consumed (Kuriyama 2006). However in the study by Shen at al 2015 black tea was found to have better correlation to improved MMSE as compared to green tea. Lastly polyphenols such as catechins in particular appear to exhibit an age related reversal of hippocampal tissue (Paulo and Assuncao 2012). This fact may account for the improvement of MMSE results among those with impaired MMSE at the start of the study (Ide 2014). L Theanine may suppress stress induced cortisone that is responsible for stress induced attenuation of hippocampal CA 1long term potentiation. Therefore both polyphenols as well as L theanine have a beneficial effect on the hippocampus which is an organ responsible for memory. This preventive effect of L theanine brings about improved recognition memory. (Tamano H et al 2013).

Other benefits of green tea on the brain include

1. Beneficial changes in reward and learning.

Catechins are known to be protective against neuro-degeneration especially brain functions involved in learning and memory.

2. Improvement of attention through increased PPI.

Attentional improvements were brought about by L Theanine. L theanine resembles chemically the neurotransmitter glutamate that is responsible for inflow and out flow of information from the dorsolateral prefrontal cortex. L theanine is thus able to act on glutamate receptors.

The beneficial effect of L theanine on PPI has been reproduced in a study using memantine. A low dose of memantine which acts as a NMDA receptor antagonist at a low dose leads to increased PPI and a dopamine agonist at high dose leads to opposes these NMDA effects (Ota et al 2014) This compound is also known to increase learning and memory through this mechanism.

3. Improvement of depressive symptoms.

Green tea was shown to decrease scores of Hamilton depression rating scale (HAMD) and Montgomery depression rating scale (MADRS) compared to placebo in the study by Zhang et al 2013. These findings have been replicated by Phamn et al 2014. In this study, those who consumed less than one cup of tea a day were compared to those who consumed more than 4 cups per day. Those with higher consumption were noted not to be depressed. It is likely that L- theanine plays a role in this.

MEDITERRANEAN DIET

Mediterranean diet is a choice of foods based on the traditional foods and drinks surrounding the Mediterranean sea. Mediterranean lifestyle includes foods, activities, meals with friends and family and wine in moderation with meals. The diet includes whole grained pasta, with vegetables and Greek salad etc. The diet may vary between these countries and also regions within a country. Differences in culture, ethnic background, religion, economy and agricultural production result in different diets.

Features of the Mediterranean diet are as follows

People from the Mediterranean area get plenty of exercise

Eat mostly plant based food like fruits, vegetables, whole grain, legumes and nuts. Nuts, beans, legumes and seeds are good sources of healthy, fats, proteins and fiber. Most of the fats are unsaturated. They are not eaten in large amounts because nuts are high in calories.

Vegetables are drizzled with olive oil. Raw vegetables such as tomatoes and olive are also eaten.

Mediterranean diet, replaces butter with healthy fats such as olive oil and cannola oil. Bread is dipped in olive oil.

Using herbs and spices instead of salt to flavour foods.

Eating fish and poultry at least twice a week.

The Mediterranean people drinking resveratrol in moderation.

Fats

This diet chooses healthier fats. Hydrogenated fats and trans fats are not encouraged. MUFA and PUFA are the preferred choice. Olive oil helps to reduce LDL cholesterol levels. Extra virgin and virgin olive oils have higher levels of antioxidants. Canola oil contains linolenic acid a type of omega 3 fatty acid which lowers triglyceride levels, decrease clotting of blood, decrease sudden heart attack, improve health of blood vessels and help moderate blood pressure.

Cheese and yogurt.

The calcium in cheese and yogurt is important for bone and heart health. Low fats and non -dairy products are preferable.

Fish and shellfish are important sources of healthy protein. Most rich in essential heart healthy omega 3 FF such as tuna, sardines and salmon. Shellfish and crustaceans including mussels, clams and shrimp have similar benefits. Fish and shellfish are not typically battered and fried. Fish is generally grilled.

Eggs

Eggs are a good source of high quality protein. Eggs area good option for vegetarians.

Meats

Meats are eaten in small portions by the Mediterranean people. Lean cuts of meats are preferable. Poultry is a good source of lean protein. Saturated fats are avoided.

Wine

Alcohol is associated with a reduced risk of heart disease. 1-2 glasses a day for men and one glass a day for women.

Herbs

They add flavours and aromas to food. Reducing the needs to add salt or fat when cooking. They are also rich in a broad range of health promoting antioxidants.

Portion size

Because foods in the bottom section of the pyramid may be eaten in larger amounts and more frequently, portion size and frequency of consumption decline in the pyramids upper section.

Moderation

Moderation is a wiser approach. A balanced and healthy diet accommodates most food and drinks.

Healthy Lifestyle Habits

Physical activity is essential for a healthy lifestyle. Meals in the company of others. The Mediterranean diet incorporates enjoyment. Foods are eaten in the company of others and savoured not gobbled.

OKINAWA DIET

Okinawa diet is known as a longevity diet. This diet originates from the Japan and is known to be associated with long average life expectancy and low risk of developing age related diseases.

Women have a life span of 86 years and men 78 years Heart disease, stroke or cancer are not commonly found. They have the lowest incidences of these major illnesses in the world. Based on research there are 4 cardinal features and they are low calorie, regular exercise, plant based and a positive outlook. Research shows that the success of the Okinawa diet is not due to genetics but rather the good diet. They stay active and maintain a vegetable garden. The garden is a good source of healthy food and also physical activity. Because of the gardening Okinawans have a lot of vitamin D and this in turn promotes bone health. Dementia is also fairly low among the Okinawans. Even in their 90s Okinawans suffered less dementia than the populations of the world. Eating the Okinawan way is associated with less cancer, osteoporosis, dementia and numerous age associated diseases.

Features of the Okinawa diet include.

1. Eat 3 nutrients a day that are rich in calcium (2-4 portions) - this is important for bones and to prevent osteoporosis.
2. Eat 10 whole wheat grains a day (7-13 portions) that is to increase the fibre level for a day.
3. Eat 3 products per day that are rich in fish oil (Omega 3) (1-3 portions) - these fatty acids are essential for health of heart, brain and immune system.
4. Eat 10 kinds of vegetables and fruits a day (7-13 portions) - vegetables and fruits that are rich in antioxidants that can help prevent damage to the cells.
5. Eat 3 nutrients daily that are rich in flavonoids (2-4 portions)- they believe that flavonoid can fight the cancer due to its antioxidant effect.
6. Drink plenty of clear still water and tea.
7. Eat little to no meat (except fish) they prefer meat that is cooked instead of frying and roasting.
8. Eat no more than 7 eggs a week as it is high in cholesterol.
9. Be moderate with alcohol. Even better if you do not drink it at all. Except the occasional glass of resveratrol.
10. Use a multi vitamin or mineral supplement that cover 50 to 100% of the recommended daily intake to prevent vitamin deficiency.
11. Eat until 80% full. They allow 20 minutes for the stretch receptor to be activated. As 20 minutes after eating you will feel full.
12. Regular walks and life-long physical activity. Stay lean and fit.

CHAPTER 3

—— ⏀ ——

PSYCHOLOGICAL STRESS AND ITS EFFECT ON THE BRAIN

Stress is defined as any uncomfortable "emotional experience accompanied by predictable biochemical, physiological and behavioural changes" (Baum A 1990).

It is well known that stress is a necessary mechanism for survival, however, chronic or severe stress has a negative impact on the brain. Stress disrupts both the normal structure and functioning of the brain. It is however, essential to understand that the psychological impact of stress on an individual, depends on not only the severity or chronicity of the stressor, but also the perception and response of the individual, to the stressful event. The individual's perception of the event would arise from his experiences in the past, his emotional and psychological makeup, his views of himself and the world around him. Hence the perception of stress would vary from one individual to another. The impact on the individual would naturally vary too.

It is well known that stress not only increases the risk of development of mental health difficulties, but also increases the individual's risk of developing other brain disorders later.

Pathophysiology of stress on the brain

An individual's ability to learn and their memory, is affected by stress. Stress is associated with deficits of cognition, due to the high levels of glucocorticoids that result. Memory is often impaired by elevated excitatory amino acids and glucocorticoid levels, which result in the atrophy of the hippocampus.

The physiological responses to stressful stimuli, are mediated by the sympathoadrenal system and the hypothalamic pituitary adrenocortical (HPA) axis. The HPA axis is mediated by the hippocampus. Stress stimulates the release of corticotropin-releasing factor (CRF), from the hypothalamic paraventricular nucleus (PVN), into the hypophysial-portal circulation. Here adrenocorticotropin hormone (ACTH) is released from the anterior pituitary, while, glucocorticoids such as cortisol, from the adrenal glands. It is the hormonal and neuronal mechanism which work towards maintaining reasonable levels of glucocorticoids.

A neurotoxicity hypothesis supported by animal studies, have shown that long exposure to glucocorticoids, are associated with hippocampal atrophy, leading to damage to neurons. While the hippocampus is so essential for learning and memory, it is susceptible to stress, due to the presence of these glucocorticoid receptors. Other major areas of the brain that are susceptible to stress, are the prefrontal cortex and amygdala.

Stress for short periods can in fact increase learning and memory, however if stress becomes chronic, the reverse is often seen. The effects of glucocorticoids on memory are exerted by the binding of corticosteroids to two receptors in the brain: the type-1, mineralocorticoid, a high affinity receptor, which lies mostly in the hippocampus, while the type -2, glucocorticoid receptor, in the hippocampus, amygdala, and prefrontal cortex.

In order to maintain cognitive functioning, a balance of these 2 receptors is essential for memory and learning. Thus, a balance in the expression of mineralocorticoid receptors and glucocorticoid receptors, is necessary for maintaining an individual's learning and memory. In normal conditions, selective activation of type-1 receptors by mild or moderate glucocorticoid levels enhances memory, while activation of type-2 receptors by high glucocorticoid levels, would impair memory and learning.

Stress and Disorders of the Brain

Stress is associated with worsening of functional deficits, as well as structural changes of the brain. This in turn causes increased vulnerabilities to develop disorders of the brain such as Alzheimer's disease, Cushing's disease and Parkinson's disease etc. Other disorders that stress has a huge negative impact on are schizophrenia, thyroid disorders, Huntington's disease, depression as well as bipolar disorder.

In the context of mental health, acute stress can serve as precipitators of mental health conditions, while chronic stresses of life serve to perpetuate mental health conditions, such as depressive or anxiety disorders. There has been a huge wave of interest on the concept of burnout, where high stress levels have been associated with burnout among individuals. Detecting stress and burnout is valuable in order to screen and detect possible mental health difficulties.

It is well established that stress is a risk factor for the development of various diseases. The effects of stress on brain structure and function, are similar to brain disorders such as Alzheimer's disease and Parkinson's disease. These will be discussed briefly as follows.

1. Parkinson's Disease

The HPA axis has a role as being one of the etiological factors of Parkinson's disease (PD). Parkinson's disease is a neurodegenerative disorder, progressive in nature, with a multifactorial etiology. It is largely due to the loss of dopaminergic neurons from the nigrostriatal pathway. Loss of neurons, and protein accumulation are also one of the causes of PD.

Most of the cases are sporadic. However, approximately 10 % are due to genetic causes. The effects of ageing and genetic vulnerability, together with stress and environmental factors, are involved in the manifestation of this disorder. Depression too, is often associated with Parkinson's disease.

During acute stresses, dopamine is released during acute stresses, however stress that is chronic causes reductions in dopamine in areas of the brain such as prefrontal cortex, frontal cortex and nucleus accumbens. It is the combination of reduced dopamine levels caused by stress, together with an impaired dopaminergic system as seen in Parkinson's disease, that results in further aggravation. Hence the management of stress levels in elderly who are a vulnerable group, is essential.

It is well known that stress is associated with raised levels of cortisol. High cortisol is also an etiological factor for the development of PD. Cortisol levels are raised in PD patients, which is an indication of stress. Stress can increase motor symptoms of PD, as well as cause PD in later life as well. High cortisol levels also serve to accelerate the development of PD.

2. Alzheimer's disease

Alzheimer's disease (AD) is an irreversible, progressive neurodegenerative disease. In Alzheimer's disease, enhanced levels of glucocorticoids are seen. Raised glucocorticoid levels are similarly seen in chronic stress, which increase the ageing of the brain. The age associated deterioration of hippocampal neurons, interfere with the negative feedback inhibition of the HPA Axis, causing a rise in glucocorticoid levels. Hence explaining the vulnerability of these neurons, with the process of ageing.

Conclusion:

The consequences of chronic stress are grave, especially with its association with mental and emotional health difficulties, as well as disorders of the brain. Individuals with mental health difficulties are more vulnerable to develop medical conditions. Improving one's life style and and making behavioral changes, are crucial steps towards reducing stress, and improving one's well being

CHAPTER 4

DEMENTIA

This is a disease of the brain usually of a chronic progressive nature in which there is a disturbance of multiple higher cortical function including memory, thinking, orientation, comprehension, calculation, language and judgement. Consciousness is not clouded. Dementia affects ones' daily functioning a diagnosis of dementia is made only if the symptoms are persistent for at least 6 months. Frequently it is progressive in it may either be reversible or irreversible.

Differentials of dementia are

Delirium,
Learning disabilities,
Focal cerebral damage
Age related memory loss.

Types of dementias.

Reversible dementias.

Metabolic disorders
Vitamin B 12 deficiency
Hypothyroidism

Irreversible dementias.

Alzheimers disease
Vascular dementia
Pick's Disease
Parkinson's Disease
Huntington's Disease
Creutzfeldt- Jakob disease
Human Immunodeficiency Virus
Multiple sclerosis
Hydrocephalus

Who is at risk of developing dementia.

1. Alzheimers disease

Those who have a strong family history of Alzheimer's dementia.

2. Vascular dementia

Those who have prolonged hypertension, uncontrolled diabetes, atrial fibrillation, or a history of transient ischaemic attacks.

3. Parkinson's demetia

Those who have repeated head trauma.

4. Depression and dementia
5. Those who have chronic depression are [predisposed to developing dementia.

Exposure to prion proteins through human growth factor, corneal transplantation or the consumption of BSE infected meat.

AGE SPECIFIC PREVALENCE RATES OF DEMENTIA

Age range (years)				
31-60	61-70	71-80	81-90	90+
0.1	1.5	5.0	25	35

An explanation to the above table, If there are 100 people aged between 90 and above then 35 of them will have one of the types of dementia.

Symptoms of dementia

Patients in the early stages may be aware of their declining memory and their functional ability. This can cause depression and anxiety. However this awareness is lost as the disease progresses. Leading to a denial of the problem and frequently refusal of help.

Other examples of dementia symptoms

Going upstairs and then forgetting why.
Going shopping and not buying all the required items.
Becoming lost on a half familiar route.
Failing to pass on telephone messages.
Repeating the same question.
Forgetting conversations that took place.
Becoming lost in a familiar place.
Problems to remember new information.

MINI MENTAL STATE EXAMINATION

The first such test was published in 1975 in a paper by Marshall F Folstein, his wife Susan Folstein and Paul Mc Hugh (Vyas and Shree Ram 2015). The Journal Psychiatric Research wrote about it as a series of questions marked on 30 points and was used frequently in research to measure if there was any defects in the cognition (Pangman et al 2000). It was initially utilized to differentiate organic (those illnesses due to a general medical condition) from functional (due to psychiatric causes) impairment (Folstein et al 1975, Tombaugh et al 1992). It is also being used a screening tool for dementia a degenerative disease of the brain (Vyas and Shree Ram 2015). The MMSE is used to assess how bad is the illness and progression over duration of time and can be used as a tool to show the effectiveness of treatment that is instituted.

Among the advantages of MMSE are that it requires no detailed training. It is both a valid and reliable scale. It takes only 10 minutes to do (Tuijl et al 2012). The MMSE can be used to differentiate between the different dementias. Those with Alzheimer's disease score lower on orientation and recall compared to patients with Parkinson's, vascular or Lewy Body Dementia. Alzheimer's dementia is the most common dementia of all (Vyas and Shree Ram 2015).

Disadvantages of MMSE are that it is needs to be translated or interpreted into various languages, it is affected by chronological age and education standing. It also frequently fails to pick up minimal defects and cognitive deficiencies and it has only a few items that tests visuospatial ability (Tomburgh 1992).

CHAPTER 5

COMORBID CONDITIONS THAT CONTRIBUTE TO THE AGING OF THE BRAIN

Individuals with dementia often have comorbid medical conditions. The presence of these comorbidities themselves, serve to further impair the individual's cognitive functioning. Therefore, dementia cannot be treated as an isolated condition, but one which has multiple comorbidities, that affect the quality of life and the cognitive functioning and needs to be looked out for.

The comorbidities of dementia are common, and usually preventable. Unfortunately, they are often only detected at a later stage, and less likely to be treated, as compared to people without dementia. People with dementia forget to take their medication, take the wrong doses, and hence this further exacerbates their comorbid disorders, resulting in serious consequences. Some of the commonly associated disorders are further discussed.

1) Depression

Depression is the most common psychiatric manifestation seen in patients with dementia. The fact that many of the symptoms of both dementia and depression overlap, makes detection and treatment difficult.

Studies have demonstrated a high prevalence of depression in patients with dementia, ranging from 8 % to 30% (Enache, D et al (2011), Huang, C Q et al (2011), Lyketsos, C G (2010). Depression itself proves to be a risk factor for dementia, where Individuals who develop depression later in life, have a twofold risk of developing Alzheimer's disease at a later point in time. As these comorbid disorders can affect the already cognitively impaired individual, careers need to be vigilant to watch out for abrupt declines in cognition, confusion or abrupt changes in symptomology.

Treatment of depression would involve family members or caretakers, together with a mental state assessment and exploring of psychosocial stressors that could be impacting the individual with Dementia. It needs to be remembered that changes in personality and increased sensitivity, irritability and at later stages the emergence of psychotic symptoms, all contribute to the depressive state of the person. Therefore, the detection and management of depression is imperative.

Management would also involve the healthy lifestyle habits such as good nutrition, which has been shown to be an essential component in the treatment of depression. Physical activity, socializing and interacting with others, undertaking mentally stimulating activities are all essential components of management.

As dementia progresses, the individual requires more assistance and care in terms of their activities of daily living, such as bathing, dressing, etc. the individual becomes increasingly dependent on the caregiver, and the emergence of behavioural and psychological symptoms of dementia, (BPSD). The role of the caregivers become increasingly difficult, and often caregivers themselves experience caregiver burden, and are themselves at risk of developing depression. The mental health needs of caregivers themselves needs to be addressed during clinical visits. If the caregiver's wellbeing is not looked after, this can cause negative impact on the care of this already vulnerable individual with dementia.

2) Diabetes

Studies have demonstrated that prevalence rates of diabetes amongst people with dementia are high, with study results varying from 6% to 39% (Bunn 2014). The risk of developing dementia is increased, when the individual has Type 2 diabetes.

The consumption of sugary and fatty foods increase the risk of Type 2 diabetes. Often individuals with dementia, they individual experiences changes in dietary habits, and hence they are predisposed to an increased risk of diabetes. Exercise is essential as it assists in reducing the risk of diabetes. The development of diabetes in the individual with dementia, poses great difficulties for the patient, as he is now faced with a new disorder.

Regular annual check-ups are important, where blood glucose levels, cholesterol levels and vision of the individual is monitored. The patient has to adapt to regimes of blood sugar checking and insulin administration.

3) Urinary Tract Infections

Urinary tract infections (UTIs), are one of the most common infections in the older population. They contribute to increased hospitalization, and pose increased risk of mortality. A study reported that 41.3% of people with dementia, had admissions to hospital due to urinary tract infections (Sampson 2009)

In elderly patients, they often missed and detected late, presenting as delirium. The infection aggravates the already declining cognitive process of the patient. Diagnosing UTI can be challenging, as individuals with dementia in advanced stages, have difficulty communicating and expressing their difficulties and symptoms.

Their vulnerability to the development of UTIs, are multifactorial. Dehydration, poor hygiene, and urinary retention are common preventable causes of UTI's. Comprehensive care plans which incorporate a structured plan of the patient's day, would need to be developed. The consumption of sufficient fluids each day, adequate washing of genitals, encouraging the patient to go to the toilet, would need to be developed, together with the caregiver. This would need to be part of the treatment plan at clinic visits.

Conclusion

Being diagnosed with dementia, greatly affects the detection and management of other comorbid medical conditions. This being due to the cognitive impairment and significant vulnerabilities of the patient. Other diseases such as cerebrovascular disease, congestive heart failure, etc are also associated with dementia. The discussion of these additional disorders, are beyond the scope of discussion of this chapter. They are nevertheless essential to detect, and manage. A holistic approach is necessary in the management of dementia and its comorbidities, as the comorbid disorder can have a more disabling impact than the dementing process itself.

References

Baum, A (1990). Stress, Intrusive Imagery, and Chronic Distress, "Health Psychology, Vol.6, pp. 653-675.

Bunn, Fetal (2014). Comorbidity and dementia: a scoping review of the literature. BMC Medicine, 12:192.

Chacko, S., Thambi, P., Kuttan, R., Nishigaki., 2010. Beneficial effects of green tea: a literature review. Chin Med., (5),13-21.

Cromwell, H.C., 2008. Sensory gating: A translational effort from basic to clinical science. Clin EEG and Neurosci., 39(2), 69-72.

De Mejia EG, Ramirez-Mares MV, Puangpraphant S., 2009. Bioactive components of tea: Cancer, inflammation and behavior. Brain Behav Immun, 23, 721-731.

Dementia Fact sheet. WHO. INT. April 2012.

Derek, E., and Jonides, J., 2014. Frontal–Medial Temporal Interactions Mediate Transitions among Representational States in Short-Term Memory. The J of Neurosci, 34(23),7964 –7975.

Derek, E., Joshua, B., Askren, M., Marc, B.,Emre, D, Adam, K., and Jonides, J. 2015. A Meta-analysis of Executive Components of Working Memory. Cerebral Cortex, 23 (2), 264-282.

Dominic B, Giorgia F, Franca F, Carla M. 2015. Structural Properties of Green Tea Catechins. J Phys Chem. Ahead Of Print.

Dudai, Yadin 2002. Memory from A to Z: Keywords, concepts, and beyond. 1ˢᵗ ed Oxford, UK: Oxford University Press.

Enache, D et al (2011). Depression in dementia: epidemiology, mechanisms, and treatment. Curr Opin Psychiatry; 24: 461-472.

Fisone, G, Borgkvist, A., Usiello, A., 2004. Caffeine as a psychomotor stimulant: mechanism of action. Cell. Mol. Life Sci., 61, 857-872.

Folstein, M.,Folstein, S., McHugh, P. 1975. ""Mini-mental state". A practical method for grading the cognitive state of patients for the clinician". J Psych Res, 12 (3), 189–98.

Fredholm, B., Bättig, K., Holmén, J., Nehlig, A., Zvartau, E., 1999. Actions of Caffeine in the Brain with Special Referece to Factors That Contribute to Its Widespread Use. Pharmacol. Rev.,51, 83-133.

Harbowy, M. E., and Douglas A. 1997. Tea Chemistry. Crit Rev in Plant Sci.,16, (5): 415–480.

Huang, C Q et al (2011). Cognitive function and risk for depression in old age: a meta-analysis of published literature. Int Psychogeriatr, 23: 516-525.

Isah T.2015. Rethinking Ginkgo biloba L.: Medicinal uses and conservation. Pharmacogn Rev.; 9(18):140-8.

Kuriyama, S., Hozawa, A., Ohmori, A., Shimazu, T., Matsui, T., Ebihara, S., Awata, S., Nagatomi, R., Arai, H. and Tsji, I. 2006. Green tea consumption and cognitive function: a cross-sectional study from the Tsurugaya Project 123.Am J Clin Nutr., 83(2),355-61.

Lardner AL. 2014. Neurobiological effects of the green teaconstituent theanine and its potential role in the treatment of psychiatric and neurodegenerative disorders. Nutr. Neurosci.,17(4),145-155.

Lyketsos, C G (2010). The interface between depression and dementia: where are we with this important frontier? Am J Geriatr Psychiatry, 18: 95-97.

Lorist MM, Tops M. Caffeine, fatigue, and cognition. Brain Cogn. 2003; 53: 82-94.

Luria A. R.. 1976. The Working Brain: An Introduction To Neuropsychology. 1st ed. USA.

Moeko, N., Sohshi, Yuki., Chiaki, D., Yoshihisa, I., Miharu, S., Kazuo, I., Masami, Y., Kimiko, A., Kiyonobu, K., Hiroyuki, N. and Masahito, Y.,2014. Consumption Of Green But Not Black Tea Or Coffee, Is Associated With Reduced Cognitive Decline. PloS One, 9(5),e 96013.

Nathan, P., Lu, K. Gray, M., Oliver, C. 2006. "The Neuropharmacology of L-Theanine(N-Ethyl-L-Glutamine)". J of Herbal Pharmacol., 6 (2), 21–30.

Nobre, A, Rao, A., Owen, G.,2008. L-theanine, a natural constituent in tea, and its effect on mental state. Asia Pac J Clin Nutr.,17, Suppl 1:167-8.

Ota, M., Wakabayashi, C., Matsuom, J., Kinoshita, Y., Hori, H., Sasayama, D., Teraishi, T., Obu, S., Ozawa, H., Kunugi, H.,2014. Effect Of L Theanine on Sensorimotor gating in healthy human subjects. Psych Clin Neurosci.,68(5), 337-43.

Pangman, VC; Sloan, J; Guse, L. (2000). "An Examination of Psychometric Properties of the Mini-Mental State Examination and the Standardized Mini-Mental State Examination: Implications for Clinical Practice". Applied Nursing Res 13 (4): 209–213.

Randi, C.M. and Robert, S. 2014. Language Production and Working Memory. The Oxforf Handbook Of Language Production. 1st ed Oxford. Oxford Press.

Reygaert WC. 2014. The antimicrobial possibilities of green tea. Front Microbiol., 20,(5),434.

Sampson, Eetal (2009). Dementia in the acute hospital: prospective cohort study of prevalence and mortality. Br J Psychiatry, 195(1).

Susana, C., Elisabeth, C, Petronila, R., Irene, R., Susana, R, Alica, S. 2006. The effect of green tea in oxidative stress. Clin Nutr; 25(5), 790-796.

Tombaugh, T.N, McIntyre, N.J. 1992. "The Mini Mental State Examination: A comprehensive review". JAGS 40: 922–935.

Tuijl, J., Scholte, E., de Craen, A., van der Mast, R. 2012. "Screening for cognitive impairment in older general hospital patients: comparison of the six-item cognitive test with the Mini-Mental State Examination". Int J Geriatr Psych., 27, 755–762.

Tze-Pin, N., Lei, F., Mathew, N., Ee, H., and Keng B.,2008. Tea Consumption and Cognitive Impairment and Decline In Older Chinese Adults.,224-31.

Swerdlow, N., Weber, M., Qu, Y., Light, G., Braff, D,. 2008. Realistic expectations of prepulse inhibition in translational models for schizophrenia research. Psychopharmacol. (Berl), 199, 331–388.

Vyas, JV and Shree, R. 2015. Essentials Of Postgraduate Psychiatry. 2 nd ed: Paras Publisher, pg 145.

Wakabayashi, C., Numakawa, T., Ninomiya, M., Chiba, S., Kunugi, H., 2012. "Behavioral and molecular evidence for psychotropic effects in L-theanine". Psychopharmacol (Berl.), 219 (4),1099–109.

William, J, Miline, JS. 1978. Research methods in aging. Text Book of Geriatric Medicine and Gerontology. 2nd ed., New York, Churchill Livingstone.

William, M. 1943. Dictionary of Bio-Chemistry and Related Subjects. 1 st ed: Philosophical Library.

World Population Ageing, 1950-2050 (United Nations publication, Sales No. E.02.XIII.3)

Yamada, T., Terashima, T., Wada, K., Ueda, S., Ito, M., Okubo, T., Juneja, L., Yokogoshi, H.,2007. "Theanine, r-glutamylethylamide, increases neurotransmission concentrations and neurotrophin mRNA levels in the brain during lactation". Life Sci., 81 (16), 1247–55.

Yung-Sheng, L., Yao-Jen, T., Jyh-Shyan, T., Jen-Kun, L.,2003. Factors affecting the level of tea polyphenols and catchins in tea leaves. Food Chem. J Agric Food Chem,51 (7),1864-73.

Printed in the United States
By Bookmasters